PICTURE LIBRARY

PENGUINS

PENGUINS

Norman Barrett

Franklin Watts

New York London Sydney Toronto

© 1991 Franklin Watts

Franklin Watts Inc
95 Madison Avenue
New York, N.Y. 10016

Designed by
Barrett and Weintroub

Library of Congress Cataloguing-in-Publication Data

Barrett, Norman S.
    Penguins/Norman Barrett.
       p. cm. — (Picture library)
    Summary. Depicts the habitats, feeding habits, life cycle, and
different species of penguins.
    ISBN 0-531-14114-4 (lib.) / ISBN 0-531-15613-3 (pbk.)
    1. Penguins—Juvenile literature. [1. Penguins.] I. Title.
II. Series.
QL696.S473B37 1991
598.4′41—dc20

90-32151
CIP AC

Research by
Deborah Spring

Photographs by
Survival Anglia
Victorian Tourist Commission
Sea World
N.S. Barrett
Bodleian Library

Illustration by
Rhoda and Robert Burns

Technical Consultant
Michael Chinery

Contents

Introduction

Penguins are birds that live in the water and on land. They cannot fly, but they are excellent swimmers.

There are several kinds of penguins. They live in both warm and cold climates, but only in waters and lands south of the equator.

Penguins spend most of their lives in the oceans. They live on the land only when laying their eggs and raising their young.

△ A penguin jumping into the sea looks almost as if it is flying. But penguins cannot really fly. Their wings have been converted into flippers, which they use for swimming.

Penguins are sociable animals and live and play together. They nest in colonies called rookeries. Some of these rookeries have as many as a million birds.

On land, penguins walk with a comical, waddling movement. They are very popular in zoos, but it is difficult to keep them in captivity. They easily catch diseases and die.

△ A colony of king penguins, some with their brown-furred chicks. Most of the adult penguins have an egg on their feet, covered by a thick fold of skin to keep it warm. Penguins take care of their young on land. They bring them fish until they are old enough to take care of themselves.

Looking at penguins

The king penguin is adapted both to its life underwater and to the cold of its Antarctic habitat.

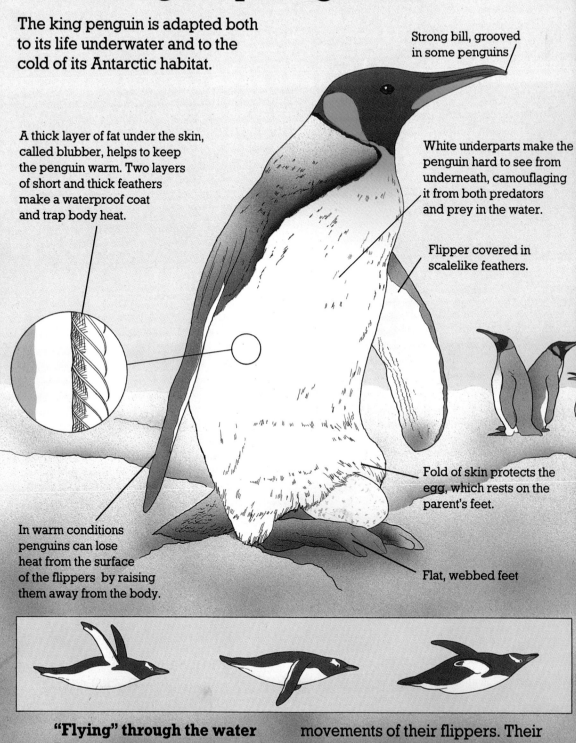

Strong bill, grooved in some penguins

A thick layer of fat under the skin, called blubber, helps to keep the penguin warm. Two layers of short and thick feathers make a waterproof coat and trap body heat.

White underparts make the penguin hard to see from underneath, camouflaging it from both predators and prey in the water.

Flipper covered in scalelike feathers.

Fold of skin protects the egg, which rests on the parent's feet.

In warm conditions penguins can lose heat from the surface of the flippers by raising them away from the body.

Flat, webbed feet

"Flying" through the water Penguins propel themselves through the water with "flying" movements of their flippers. Their legs are used as rudders, for steering.

AFRICA

9

9   Prince Edward Is
     2,4,7   Crozet Is
                      2,4,7
                                    Amsterdam Is
                                    6
Gough Is, 6   Kerguelen Is
                     2,4,6,7   Paul Is, 6

Tristan
da Cunha, 6   Bouvet Is, 5,7   Heard Is
                                            2,4,5,7

          South Sandwich Is
          2,5,7
South   ANTARTICA
Georgia   1,2,3,4,5,6
2,4,5,7
                                                            8
          South Shetlands
          South Orkneys   AUSTRALIA
Falklands 4,5,6,7
4,6,7,11
          Staten Is   Balleny Is, 4   Tasmania
11   2,4,11   8
S. AMERICA   Macquarie Is
          6   Peter Is   2,4,6
11   4
10
    Juan Fernandez   Campbell Is, 6   Auckland Is, 6
    10   South Island
                  Antipodes Is, 6   8
                  Bounty Is, 6   NEW
Galapagos, 12   ZEALAND

                  Chatham Is
                  8

Where penguins live

All penguins live in the Southern
Hemisphere. They inhabit areas of the
oceans reached by the cool Antarctic sea
currents. They breed on numerous islands
and on coastal areas of continents.

1. Emperor	7. Macaroni
2. King	8. Little
3. Adelie	9. Jackass
4. Gentoo	10. Peruvian
5. Chinstrap	11. Magellanic
6. Rockhopper	12. Galapagos

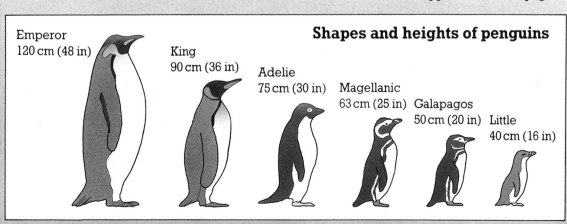

Shapes and heights of penguins

Emperor
120 cm (48 in)

King
90 cm (36 in)

Adelie
75 cm (30 in)   Magellanic
                63 cm (25 in)   Galapagos
                                50 cm (20 in)   Little
                                                40 cm (16 in)

9

Kinds of penguins

There are at least 16 different species (kinds) of penguins. Many people think of penguins as being Antarctic animals, but only two species are truly creatures of this icy continent – the emperor and the adelie.

Other species live around Antarctica. Penguin colonies are also found in Australia, New Zealand, South Africa, and South America.

△ The emperor penguin lives only in the Antarctic. It goes ashore to breed and nests on the sea ice. It has patches of orange-yellow under its head.

▷ The rockhopper penguin has a crest of yellow feathers. It is smaller than the other crested penguins and has red eyes. It breeds in rookeries on rocky coastlines.

Penguins have stocky bodies and short legs. They have short, thick feathers, white on their belly and black at the back. Some species have crests of feathers on their heads.

Most species of penguins are friendly creatures and trusting towards people. But rockhopper and chinstrap penguins can be aggressive and will attack intruders.

▷ A chinstrap penguin and chick on their nest of stones. Chinstraps look like adelies, but have a thin black line (the chinstrap) across their throats. They have very screeching voices.

▽ A fiordland crested penguin keeping its chick warm. These penguins make their nests in caves or under tree roots in the coastal forests of New Zealand and nearby islands.

◁The little blue, sometimes called the fairy penguin, breeds mainly in southern Australia and New Zealand. It is the smallest species of penguin.

▽Magellanic penguins breed on the coasts of southern South America and the Falkland Islands.

△ Macaroni penguins
on South Georgia
Island, near Antarctica.
They have a bright
orange, drooping crest.

▷ The Galapagos
penguin is the rarest
species. A thousand or
two of these birds
breed on the Galapagos
Islands, in the Pacific
Ocean, near the
equator.

Life of penguins

Penguins spend most of their lives in the oceans. They seem to fly through the water. When they need to breathe, they "fly" up to the surface, often leaping clear of the water to draw fresh breath.

They live mainly on small fish, cuttlefish and shrimplike creatures called krill.

Penguins come out of the water only to breed. They move about clumsily on land, in short, waddling steps. They often slide on ice.

▽ Penguins enjoy swimming, even in shallow waters. On the surface, they swim like ducks. Their only enemies, apart from humans, are certain kinds of seals and skuas, birds that attack their eggs and chicks.

△ The graceful swimming action of a penguin in the water. Most penguins can keep up a steady speed of between 7 and 10 km/h (4–6 mph), and can go twice as fast in short bursts. They are strong enough to swim in very rough seas.

▷ A penguin leaps out of the water to land on an ice floe.

◁Somebody has to take
the first plunge! These
rockhopper penguins
and fully grown chicks
will soon follow the
leader into the water.

Most kinds of
penguins jump into the
sea, but rockhoppers
get their name because
they seem to enjoy
jumping off small rocks,
even on land.

Penguins grow a new coat of
feathers every year. They molt, or
lose their old feathers, on land or on
pack ice.

△ A molting king
penguin (right) stands
on a carpet of feathers.

Penguins stay ashore until their
new plumage is fully developed,
because the feathers must be
watertight before they take to the
water again. The molting process
might take four weeks or more.

◁Penguins sometimes move through the water like dolphins, leaping out to breathe before plunging back again.

▽Penguins can move quickly on hard snow or ice by "tobogganing." They slide on their bellies and propel themselves along with their feet and flippers.

Breeding

Penguins go back to the same places for breeding year after year. Most species breed along coastal areas, where they can be close to the sea and their supply of food. Antarctic penguins, however, might have to travel long distances over frozen seas to reach their rookeries on the edge of the continent.

Male and female pairs usually stay together for life. They return to the same nesting place within the colony every year.

▽ A colony of king penguins on South Georgia Island. These penguins breed on islands in and around the Antarctic region.

Most penguins build their nests on the ground, among rocks and clumps of grass. Some nest in caves. Magellanic penguins dig deep burrows. The birds make their nests with whatever they can find – often just stones and grass.

Emperor penguins breed on the ice shelves where there is no material for any kind of nest.

Most penguin species lay either one or two eggs, but some lay three or even four.

△ A rockhopper carries pieces of grass in its beak for making its nest.

Most species of penguins lay their eggs three or four weeks after arriving at their rookery. The eggs have to be kept warm to allow the unborn penguins to develop. This is called incubation, and lasts for several weeks.

With most penguins, the male and female take turns at incubating the eggs and then looking after the chicks, while the other goes to the sea to feed and bring back food for the chicks.

△ A king penguin incubating its egg, which is balanced on its feet. Male and female kings share the incubation of their single egg, which hatches after about 54 days.

▷ An emperor penguin with its two-week-old chick. Newborn chicks are kept warm in the same way that the egg is incubated – balanced on the feet and covered by a thick fold of skin.

△ A rockhopper
penguin feeding its
chick. The adults only
partly digest their food,
so that they can bring it
up again for their
young.

◁ A group of 3–4-week-
old adelie chicks
huddle together in a
"crèche" for warmth
and protection. Parents,
returning with food, can
recognize their own
chicks even in crèches
of a hundred or more
chicks.

Penguins in captivity

Penguins are among the most popular animals in zoos. But they are difficult to keep alive and well in captivity. Some species of penguins die if it becomes too warm, so they must be kept in a specially refrigerated building.

Whether exhibited inside or outside, penguins need a pool of cool, clean water, deep and large enough for them to swim freely. Penguins kept in comfortable, clean conditions will breed in captivity.

▽ A variety of penguins at the Sea World exhibit in Florida. The animals live in a large indoor chamber, designed to look like their natural habitat in the Antarctic. It is cooled to below freezing, and has a pool of deep, cold water.

The story of penguins

Penguin ancestors

The very first member of the penguin family lived between 50 and 55 million years ago. It probably had the ability to fly. It is thought to have descended from the same ancestors as today's petrels and albatrosses.

As penguins adapted to life in the water, their wings changed to flippers and they lost the power of flight. This happened gradually over millions of years.

△ Over millions of years, wings changed to flippers, perfect for swimming underwater as this jackass penguin demonstrates.

Prehistoric penguins

Penguins have never lived north of the equator. Fossil remains have been found in all the places where penguins live today and date back to more than 40 million years ago. Fossils of 25 million years ago tell us that a penguin

existed then that was very much like those of today. But it was much bigger, standing more than 1.7 m (5½ ft) and weighing over 100 kg (220 lb). This is about 50 cm (20 in) taller and more than twice as heavy as the fattest, healthiest emperor penguins of today.

Where penguins first lived

Penguins probably first developed around the coasts of New Zealand. They have never moved out of the Southern Hemisphere because tropical waters are too hot for them. They move into the tropics only where cold currents flow around the coasts. They cannot fly, so have no means of reaching more distant seas.

Explorers and penguins

The first Europeans to see penguins were the great explorers of the 1400s and 1500s. Bartholemew Dias, a Portuguese navigator, was the first explorer to record seeing penguins, when sailing around the south of Africa in 1488. The Magellanic penguin is named after another Portuguese explorer, Ferdinand Magellan, who first saw them in 1520.

Explorers on long sea voyages found penguins very useful as food. In 1575, the English adventurer Sir Francis Drake and his men killed 3,000 penguins in one day. They were salted and pressed, and used as meat by the sailors.

The first king penguins were seen by the British explorer Captain James Cook, who found them in 1775 on South Georgia Island.

Dumont d'Urville, leading a French expedition to the Antarctic in 1839, first found the adelie penguins, which he named after his wife Adélie.

The first specimens of emperor penguins were captured in 1842 by a British Antarctic expedition led by Captain James Clark Ross.

Several more species, including the Galapagos penguin, were discovered in the 1870s.

Exploiting the penguin

Penguins have been killed for more than their meat. Their thick layer of fat, or blubber, has been used for making oil. Their skins have also been highly prized for making such items as hats and purses. Penguin eggs have been harvested in large quantities for food.

△ Early explorers killed penguins in their thousands to provide food for hungry sailors and replenish the ships' food supplies.

Protection

Laws have been introduced over the years for the protection of penguins. The killing of penguins has been banned in Australia and New Zealand, and some islands have become sanctuaries.

The greatest danger to penguins, however, is the threat to their habitats. Spillage from oil tankers is a continuing menace to all wildlife, as is any development for commercial reasons. An international agreement, the Antarctic Treaty, was signed in 1959 to protect that region and all its wildlife. Unfortunately, many countries are still determined to mine in the area.

Facts and records

Champion divers

Penguins can stay underwater for minutes at a time and can dive to great depths. Emperor penguins have been known to reach depths of over 260 m (850 ft) and stay down for as long as 18 minutes before coming up for air.

Penguin parade

The smallest penguins are the little blue species of Australia and New Zealand. A colony of these breeds on Phillip Island, off the coast of southern Australia.

The penguins make their nests in the sand dunes, scooping out holes where the eggs will be laid. The season lasts from mid-October to the end of March, and each day at dawn hundreds of male penguins leave the rookery to go fishing in the sea. They return at dusk, with their "catch" partly digested in their crops. They always land on a small section of the beach, and make their way in line back to feed their females and chicks. This regular "penguin parade" is usually witnessed by groups of naturalists and tourists, who can only wonder at how the penguins find their way back after swimming several miles offshore.

△ A little blue penguin leads the "parade" as the males return to their rookery on Phillip Island at dusk after a day of fishing.

Ninety-day fast

The emperor penguin can go without food for longer than any other bird. Male emperors live off their body fat for about 3 months, from the time they arrive in the rookery to when their females return from the sea with food for their newly hatched chicks. During this time the males lose nearly half their body weight.

Hardy travelers

Penguins of the Antarctic sometimes have to travel great distances over ice to reach their rookeries. Many adelie rookeries are situated as much as 80 km (50 miles) from the edge of the sea ice. So millions of penguins have to walk and toboggan for 24 hours or more to reach their nesting places.